Why Trump Is Good For America

by

Joe Kerr

I0388167

Published by the Humor Department of

Great Little Book Publishing Co.
Sacramento, CA

Why Trump is Good For America.

Copyright © 2016 by Karl W. Palachuk.

Cover artwork by Eric Black.
Email: ericblak1947@gmail.com

All rights reserved.

No part of this book may be used or reproduced in any manner whatsoever without written permission.

ISBN: 978-1-942115-37-3

Note:

This is a **blank gift book**, intended to bring joy into your life. Feel free to fill the inside pages with your own thoughts and jokes.

If you would like to find more Blank books – or create your own as a gift – visit **www.BlankGiftBook.com**.

Why Trump is Good for America

Notes:

More Titles in This Series . . .

From BlankGiftBook.com

What You Should Expect from Your Ex-Wife
by Mia Culpa

The Big Guide to Honest Politicians
by Pat McCann

How to Make Women Feel Better During Menopause
by Les Moody

How to Be an Attorney and Keep Your Soul
by Sue First

The Complete Guide to Humility for MDs
by Anita Procedure

How to Find Job Security in Corporate America
by Justin Case

What Men Know About Making Women Feel Special
by Mike Easter

. . . And you can even create your own Blank Gift Book at

www.BlankGiftBook.com

www.ingramcontent.com/pod-product-compliance
Lightning Source LLC
Chambersburg PA
CBHW071532080526
44588CB00011B/1646
* 9 7 8 1 9 4 2 1 1 5 3 7 3 *